This book
celebrates:

For Lome, Joaquín, & Mico;
For mamas & for papas;
& for Jay.

- J9M

First Published in 2013 by Blood Orange Press

Printed in Malaysia by Tien Wah Press
First Edition
1 2 3 4 5 6 7 8 9 10

ISBN 978-0-9853514-0-3

oh, oh, baby BOY!

written & illustrated by

Janine Macbeth

Blood Orange Press ❦ Oakland

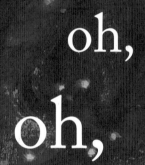

oh,

oh,

Baby Boy

sweet
sweet
Baby Boy

cutie
pie

Baby Boy

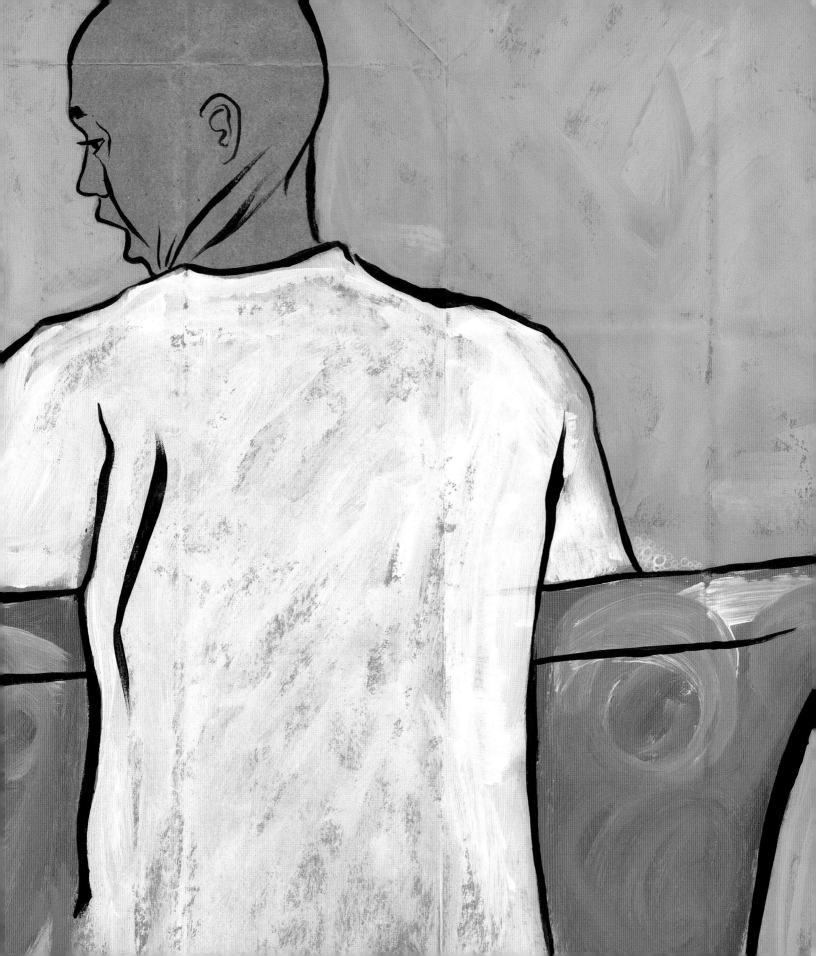

step step Baby Boy

smells of spice Baby Boy

skip

and hop

Baby Boy

bold and clear

Baby Boy

laugh

and

sing

Baby

Boy

run

and

play

Baby

Boy

explore and grow
Baby Boy

strong and kind Baby Boy

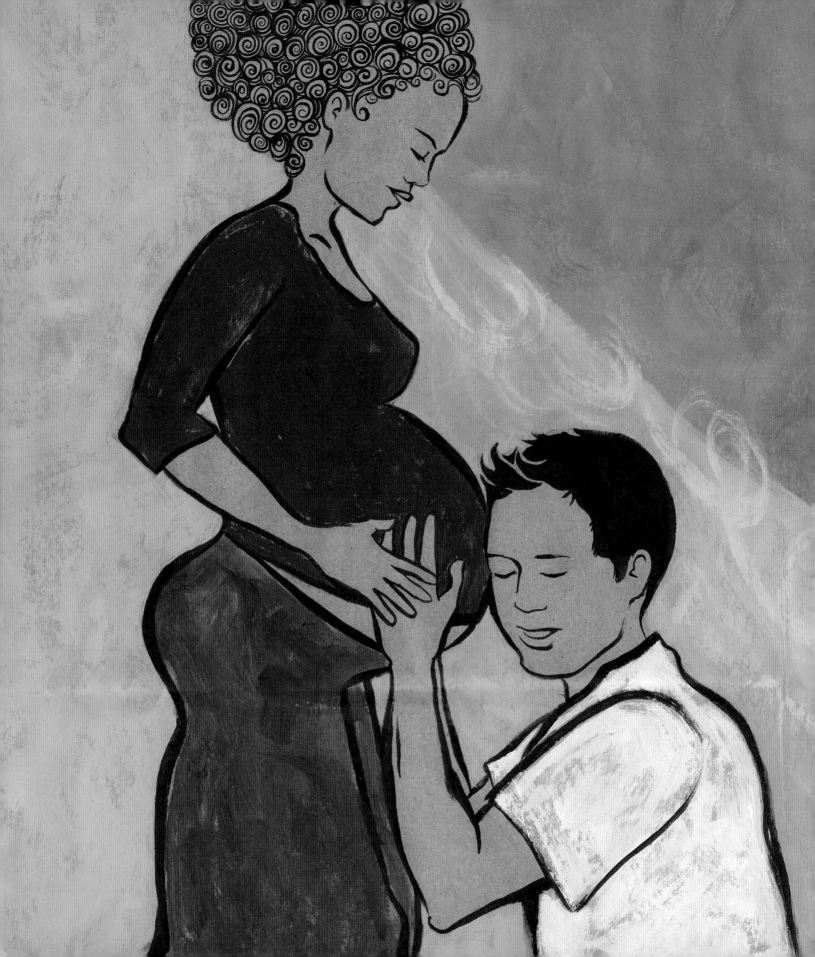

love and listen

Baby Boy

welcome
a new Baby Boy

sweet

sweet

Baby Boy

oh, oh,

Baby Boy

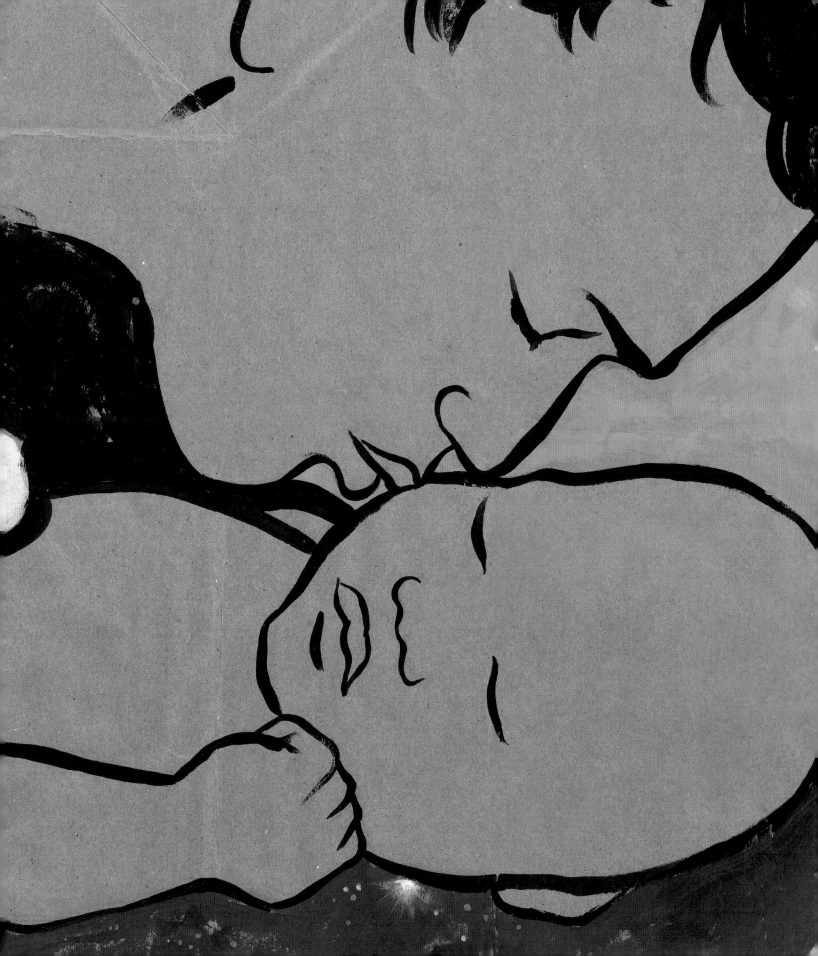

Author's Note:

In 2012, the Bureau of Labor Statistics reported that just over 70% of mothers in the United States were working moms. Whether the work is part-time, full-time, at home or outside the home, moms are increasingly becoming wage earners and entrepreneurs. The 2011 U.S. Census reported that 57.5% of kids in the United States are raised in households where both parents work. Moms are more active in the workforce than ever before; dads are more active at home than ever before. Amidst societal expectations that mothers be the primary caregiver and breadwinner as well, fathers are stepping up to do their part. A family's agility and resilience depend on it.

We're evolving into new terrains where fatherhood isn't solely an economic role that occasionally "helps" mothers. Fatherhood is increasingly becoming an equal parenting partnership, whether or not parents are romantically connected.

My husband made this book possible in more ways than one. He watched the boys on the weekends, and literally gave me the time to work on it - to fundraise for the book, write, illustrate, design, and produce it. As a mom working full-time and pursuing dreams after hours, time is a most precious resource. Even with the support of an amazing husband, it has been difficult balancing my dream to create children's books with my desire to spend time together as a family (not to mention my desire to excel in my daytime career, or be a great wife-sister-daughter-friend). In the many late night and weekend hours spent working on this book, I wondered if the end product would be worth the time I missed with my husband and boys to create it. Striking the balance has been one of my most challenging endeavors.

Patricia Clafford wrote: "The work will wait while you show the child the rainbow, but the rainbow won't wait while you do the work." The meaning and the application of these words rely on how we define *the work* and *the rainbow*.... For me, in the instance of this book, they have been one and the same.

As a mom, I see the vital role our village plays in the upbringing of our two sons. Men—and especially fathers—are integral parts of our communities. In lifting fathers up and allowing them to be more involved, more engaged, and more compassionate, we as moms give a bit of ourselves back to ourselves.

With nothing but love for the mamas,
the papas, and the babes,
J9Macbeth

Photo: Lome Aseron (Summer 2011, soon after Janine started working on *Oh, Oh, Baby Boy!*)

Special thanks to: Amber Ouye Cavala ◆ Ben Soleil Frost ◆ Candice Francis ◆ Dana Goldberg ◆ Gina Acebo ◆ Janet del Mundo ◆ Jason Sperber ◆ Joycelyn Macbeth ◆ Katherine Tillotson ◆ Robert Trujillo ◆ Sage McCollister ◆ Sandy Ratto ◆ Theresa L. Macbeth ◆ Vivian Li ◆ Yuyi Morales

And a heart-felt **thank you** to the 260 generous individuals & their families who supported this book on & off the Kickstarter platform:

Alexis Dennis ◆ Alfredo de Avila ◆ Ali Sargent ◆ Alice Ouye-Cavala ◆ Alison F ◆ Allyson ◆ Allyson Cortez ◆ Alysia Gonzales ◆ Amanda Greene ◆ Amber Ouye Cavala ◆ Amy Weimer ◆ Anastasia & Doug Chase ◆ Andrea Fellion ◆ Andy Mardesich ◆ Andy Vernon-Jones ◆ Angela Lau ◆ Annette Hinds ◆ Annu Kristipati ◆ April Yee ◆ Art Cipriano ◆ Arthur Macbeth ◆ Rashida Clendening ◆ Avis Atkins ◆ Barbara Bobrow ◆ Barbara Collins ◆ Barbara Towner ◆ Becky Smith ◆ Belen Mendoza ◆ Bernadette Houtchens ◆ Betty Kano ◆ Brendon Fong ◆ Brett Donoviel ◆ Brian Burnett ◆ Brian Washington ◆ Brooklyn Mathison ◆ Bruce Mirken ◆ Clemente Aseron ◆ C.C. Pace ◆ Candace Dodson Reed ◆ Candice Francis ◆ Carla Saporta ◆ Carmen Pearson ◆ Carol Brubaker ◆ Caroline Shek ◆ Catherine Woolf ◆ Chanelle Pearson ◆ Charlene Cossler & Alex Feng ◆ Chelsea ◆ Christina Powers ◆ Christopher Fan ◆ Cindy Imichi ◆ Claudia Paredes ◆ Connie Hebert ◆ Consuelo Velasco Montoya ◆ Corazon Sillers ◆ Corey Wiggins ◆ Corinne Pallen ◆ Corrine Lee ◆ Dana Goldberg ◆ Dana Hughes ◆ Danielle Fox

This book was made possible by a loving community of family & friends, old & new.

◆ Danny Henley ◆ Deborah Greig ◆ Denise M. Hingle ◆ Dennis Quirin ◆ Derek Markham ◆ Diana Louise Smith ◆ Diana Marie Lee ◆ Dolores Weimer ◆ Doni Ogarrio ◆ Donna Hernandez ◆ Dorothy Eng ◆ Doug Aseron ◆ Edward Pierce ◆ Elias Kass, ND LM CPM ◆ Emily Bolton Ditkovski ◆ Eric Murphy ◆ Erica Turner ◆ Erin Kilmer Neel ◆ Erin Subramanian ◆ Eve Herschkopf ◆ Farrin Sofield ◆ Felicia Hoshino ◆ Frank Aseron & Martha Ward ◆ Fumi Suzuki ◆ Gina Acebo ◆ Hatty Lee ◆ Heidi Coonfield ◆ Hongmai Nguyen ◆ Ilana Golin ◆ Indira Allegra & Kimi Mojica ◆ Irene Dea & Malcolm Collier ◆ Irmhild Liang ◆ Isaac S. Haynes ◆ Jacques-Jean Tiziou ◆ Janet Del Mundo ◆ Janet Massy ◆ Jasmine Taruc Pinson ◆ Jason Sperber ◆ Jean Chung ◆ Jeannene Zettler Rhodes ◆ Jennifer & Anne-Ellice Parker ◆ Jennifer Corey ◆ Jessica Eastwood ◆ Jessica Rose ◆ Jill Uppal ◆ Jimmy Dang ◆ Joan Fiser ◆ Joan Steinau Lester ◆ John Boring ◆ Johnnie Aseron ◆ Joyce Connor ◆ Joyce Hum Young ◆ Joycelyn Macbeth ◆ Judy Yung ◆ Julia Drees ◆ Julia Lam ◆ Julie Hedlund ◆ K. Brisbane ◆ Karen Eng ◆ Karen Sacks ◆ Karen-Lynn Bucher ◆ Katherine Tillotson ◆ Katie Nolan ◆ Katrina Alcorn ◆ Kay Fernandez Smith ◆ Kcarlyle ◆ Keli Gomez-Rodriguez ◆ Kelli Shimabukuro ◆ Kelly Lau ◆ Ken Songco ◆ Kim Brown Dye ◆ Kippy ◆ Kristen Honma ◆ Kristen Washburn ◆ Kristiana Tom ◆ Laila Reiss ◆ Lailan Huen ◆ Laura Baedeker ◆ Laura Graham ◆ Laura Paxton ◆ Laura Wong ◆ Lauren Ard ◆ Laurie Ignacio ◆ Li Aseron ◆ Liane Scott ◆ Libby Arny ◆ Libero Della Piana ◆ Linda Heneghan ◆ Lindsay Imai ◆ Lisa Giamo ◆ Lisa Louie ◆ Liz Whitted Dawson ◆ Lora Collier Chan ◆ Lori Shimonishi Low ◆ Louise Alger ◆ Maliha Williamson ◆ Mana Hayakawa ◆ Mari Rose Taruc ◆ Maria Cordero ◆ Mariah Rankine-Landers ◆ Marianne Arieux ◆ Mariel Flores Viñalon ◆ Marlowe Ward Bober ◆ Martha Ward ◆ Mattie Weiss ◆ Mary Bordewieck ◆ Mary Dee Moran ◆ Mary Lou ◆ Maxine & Hugh E. Macbeth, Jr. ◆ May Funabiki ◆ May Nee ◆ Megan Scott ◆ Melanie Cervantes ◆ Melissa Wong Nakagawa ◆ Michael Hicks ◆ Michele Raczka ◆ Milicent Johnson ◆ Mira Reisberg ◆ Miya Yoshitani ◆ Monica Carlos ◆ Monica Hernandez ◆ Muey Saetuen ◆ Nancy Lim ◆ Naomi Clark ◆ Nathan Shroyer ◆ Ney Gehman ◆ Nicole Beasley ◆ NTjane Louie & FranceDominique ◆ Orson Aguilar ◆ Paul Holcomb ◆ Per Hakansson ◆ Petra, Sean & Liam Brennan-Lippe ◆ Polly Le Grand ◆ Rashid D. Herd ◆ Renny Fong ◆ Richard Scott ◆ Rick Lee ◆ Robb D. ◆ Robert Horsford ◆ Robert Trujillo ◆ Ronald Williams, II ◆ Rosa Maria Martinez ◆ Ross Aseron ◆ Ruth Tobar ◆ Ruthie Keyes ◆ Ryan Briscoe Young ◆ Ryan Janisse ◆ Sage McCollister ◆ Saku Takano ◆ Sandra Ratto ◆ Sarah ◆ Sarah Crowell ◆ Sarah Lee Wood ◆ Sarah Strother, Ocie & Layla ◆ Sasha Werblin ◆ Seth Marlow ◆ Shaquila Smith ◆ Sharina McCants ◆ Sharon Delacruz ◆ Shiree Teng ◆ Shirley T. Ng ◆ Simón Hanukai ◆ Sonia Peña ◆ Sonya Shah ◆ Stacey Cue ◆ Stefanie Liang ◆ Stephanie Chen ◆ Stephanie Leonard ◆ Stephanie Mackley ◆ Susan Curry Sykes ◆ Susan Thurman Young ◆ Sydney Richards ◆ Tammy Johnson ◆ Tania Lee ◆ Tanner Johnson ◆ Tara Marchant ◆ Teresa Lau ◆ The StoneDancerGroup, Inc. ◆ Theresa Macbeth ◆ Thu Banh ◆ Thuan Tran ◆ Tiffany U ◆ Timothy Dunning ◆ Tina Ma ◆ Tony Steuer ◆ Tracy Kronzak ◆ Trina Villanueva ◆ Troy Christmas ◆ Vianey Nuñez ◆ Victor Henriquez ◆ Victor Stock ◆ Vincent Casalaina ◆ Virginia Harmon ◆ Vivian Li ◆ Winter King ◆ Yoly Petra Stroeve ◆ Young Whan ◆ Yvonne Kuah